For Beatrice & Tommaso, who we love to celebrate birthdays with.

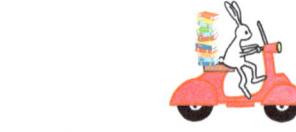

H.P. Gentileschi Publishing House
Austin - Rome

www.hpgentileschi.com

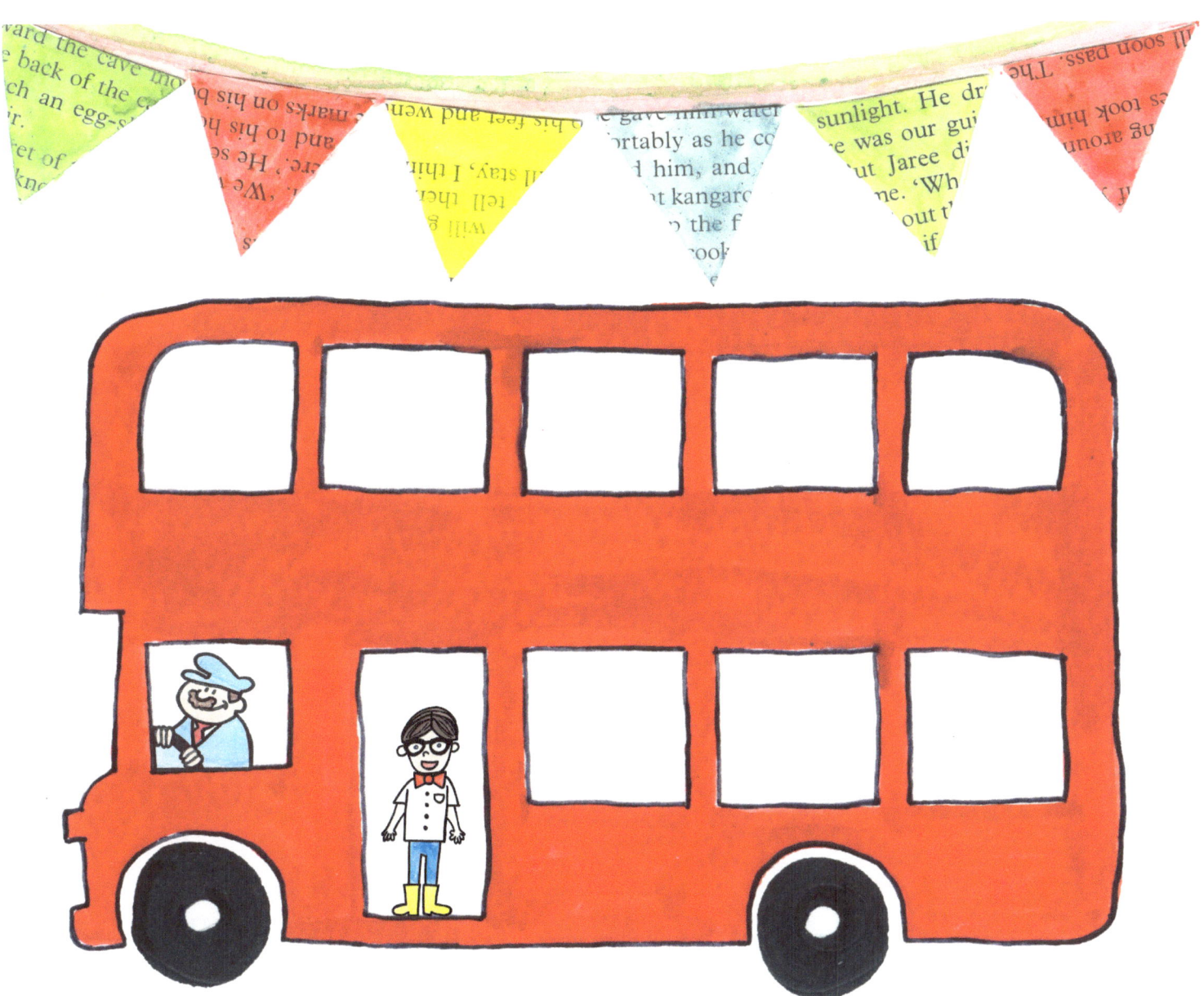

There is a boy on a bus.

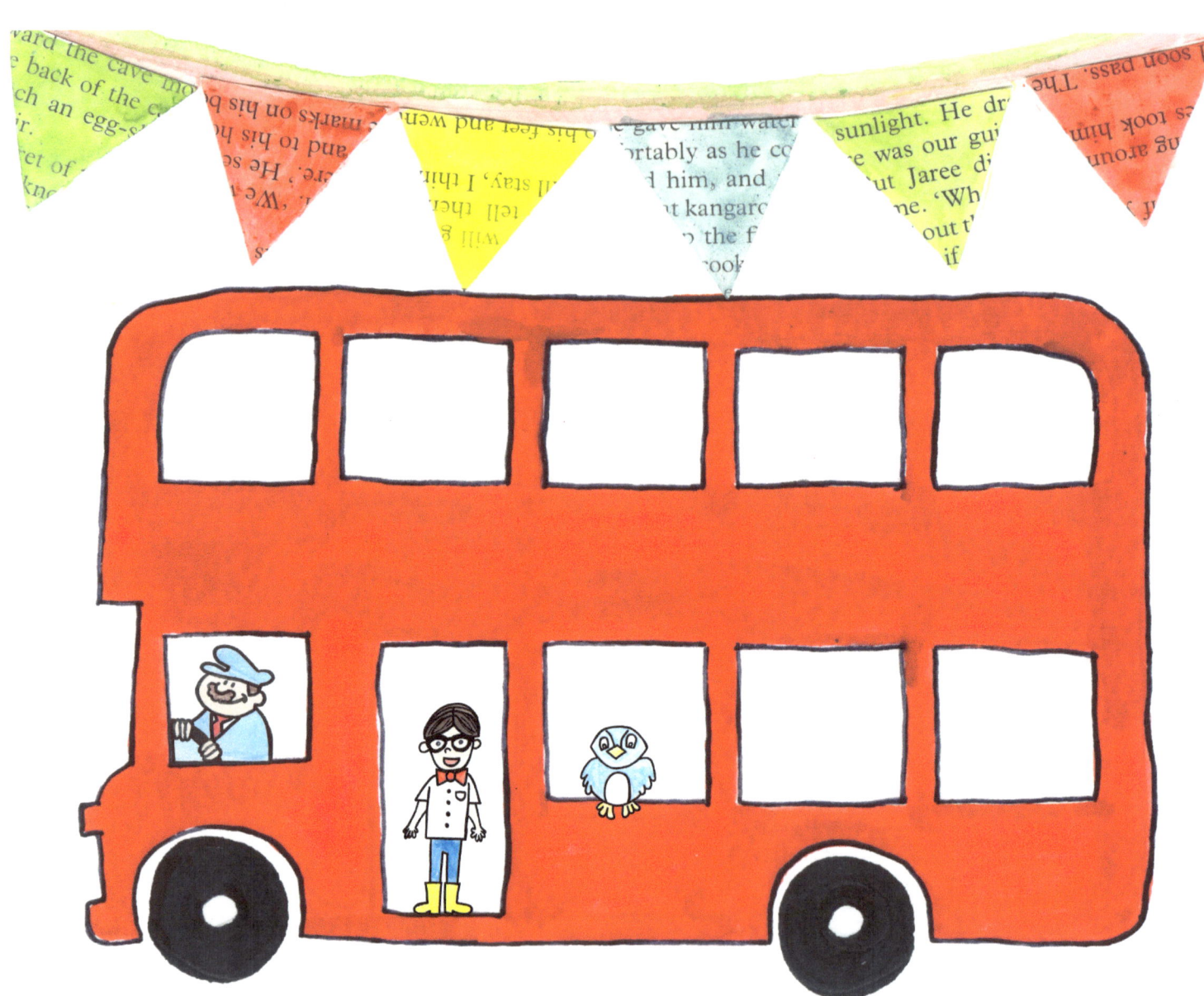

There is a boy and a bird on a bus.

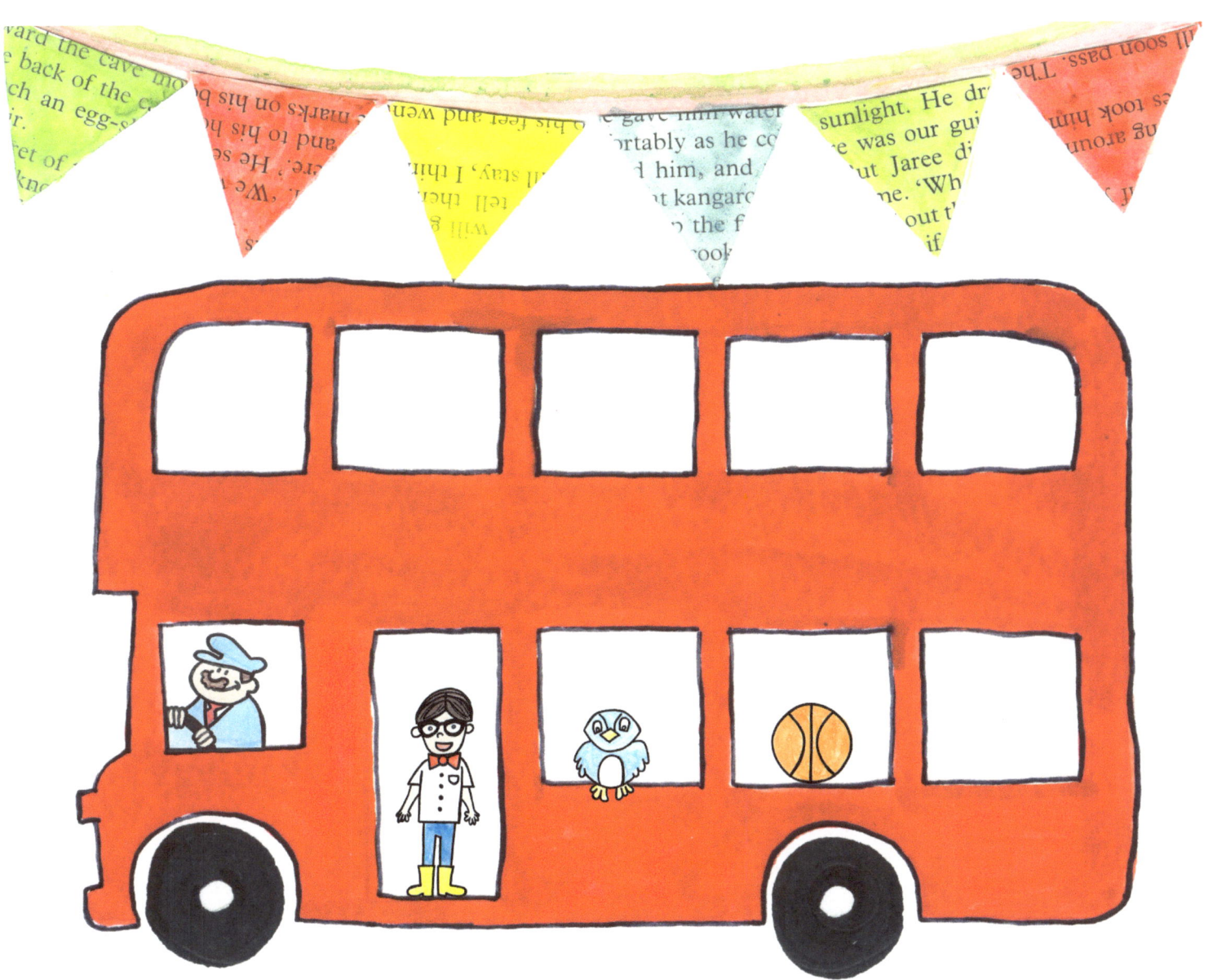

There is a boy, a bird and a ball on a bus.

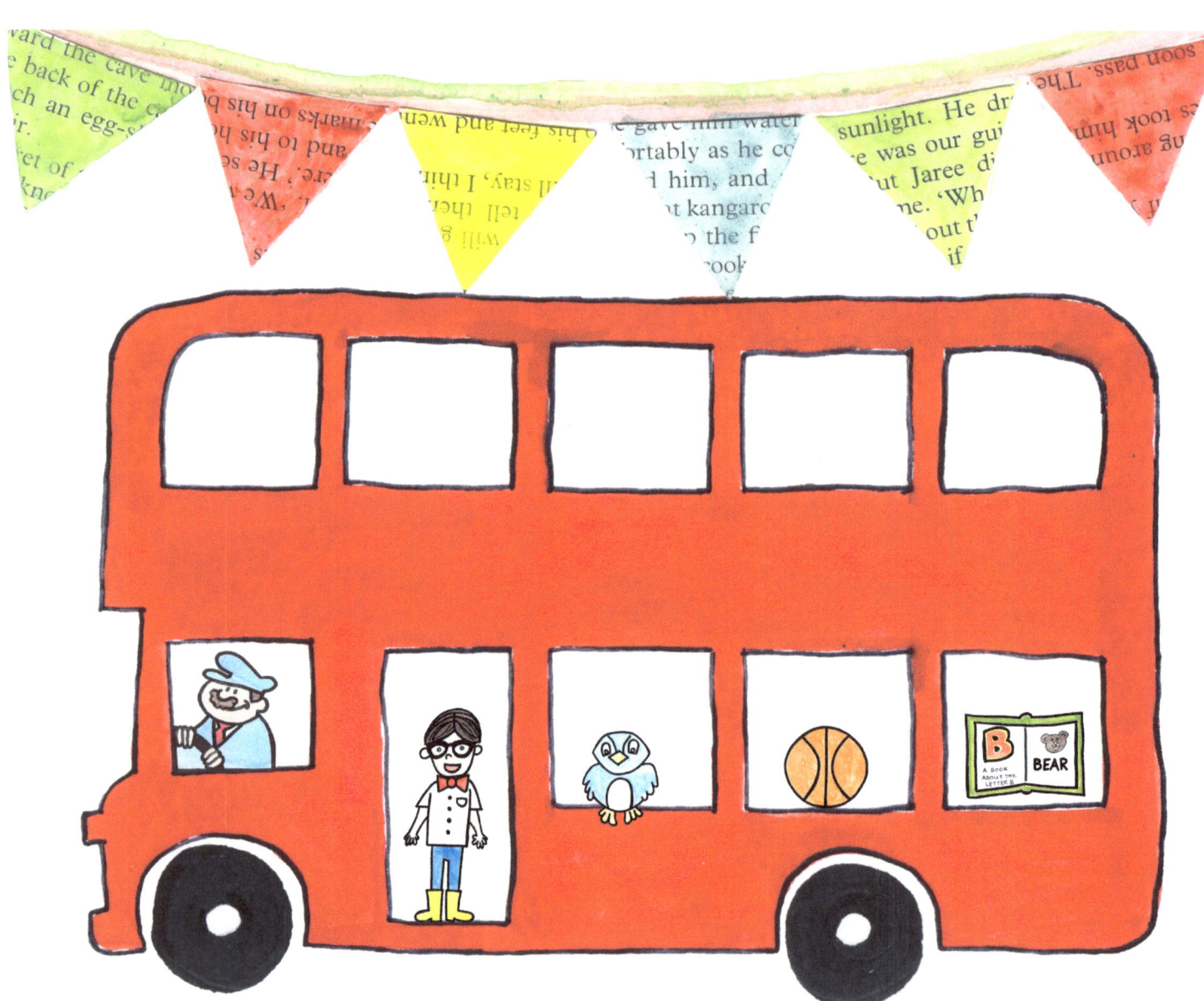

There is a boy, a bird,
a ball and a book on a bus.

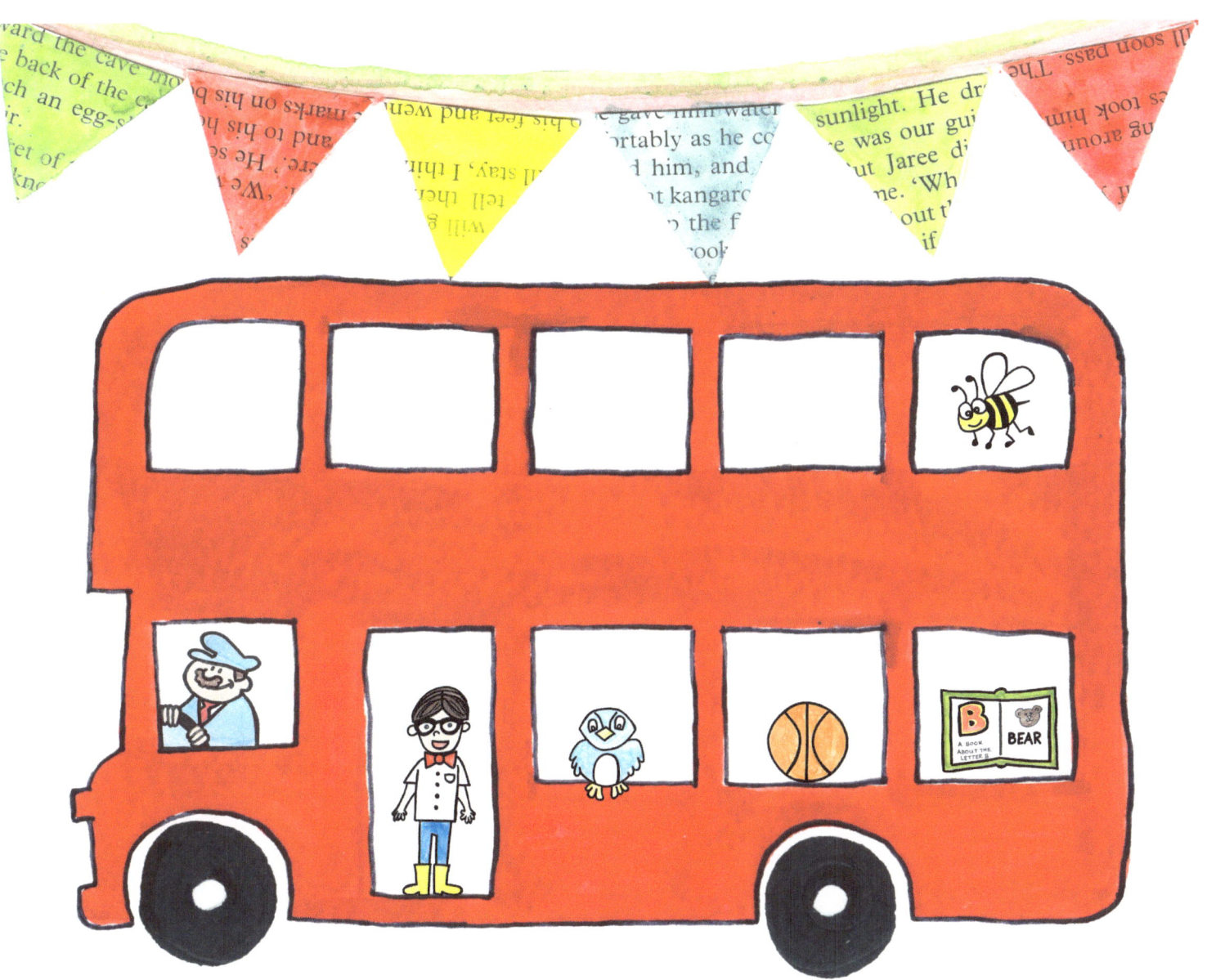

There is a boy, a bird,
a ball, a book and a bee on a bus.

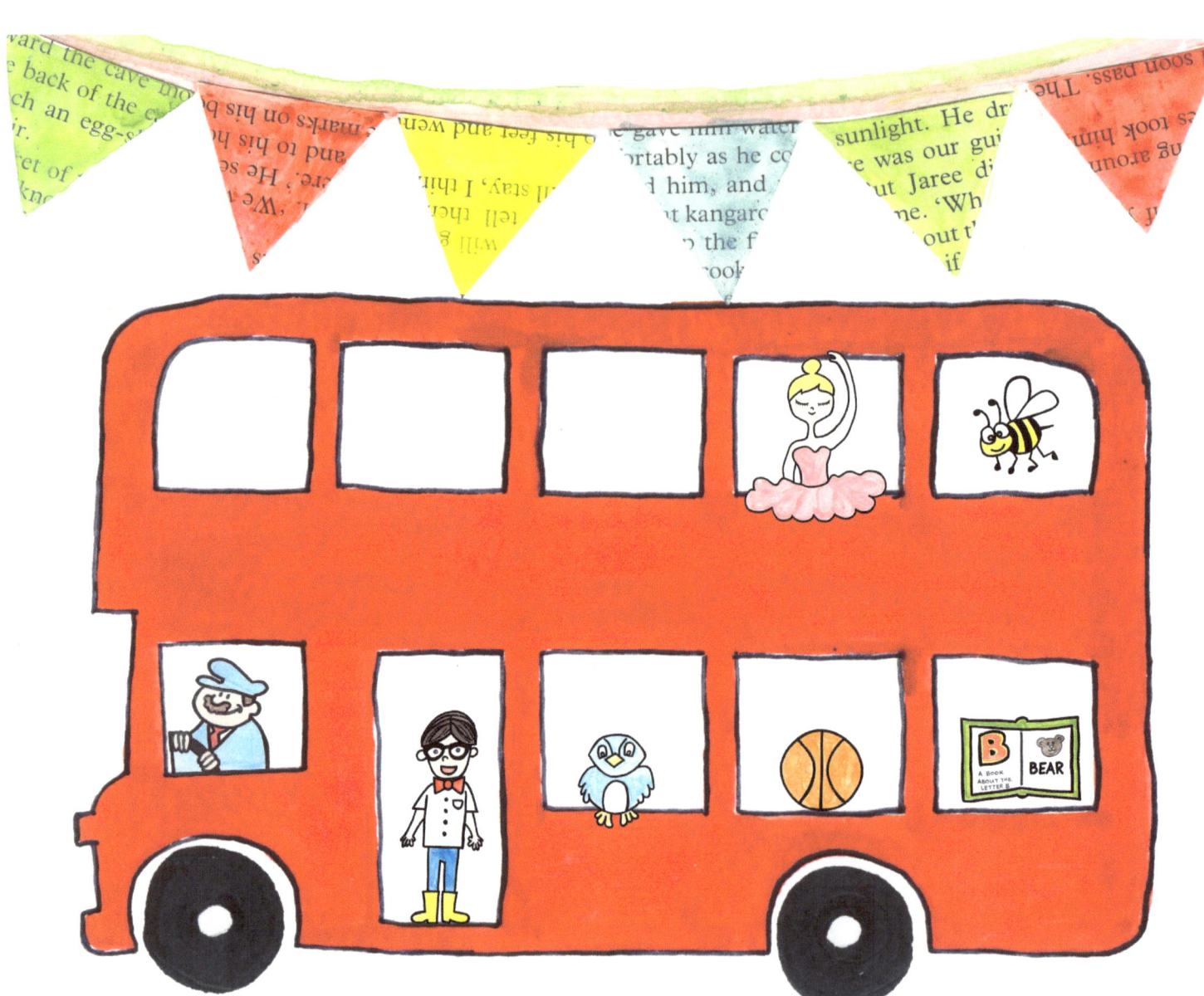

There is a boy, a bird, a ball, a book, a bee and a ballerina on a bus.

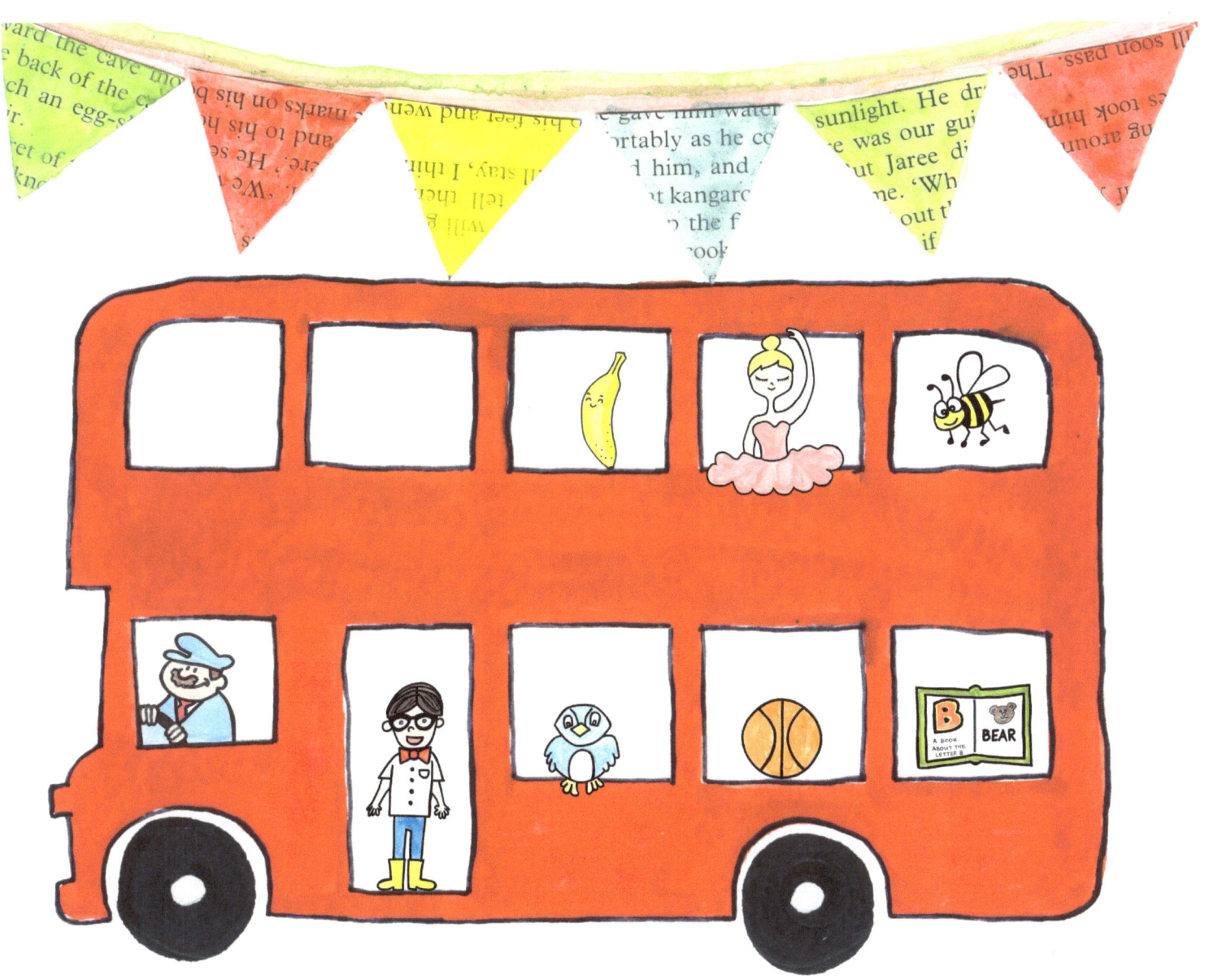

There is a boy, a bird, a ball, a book, a bee, a ballerina and a banana on a bus.

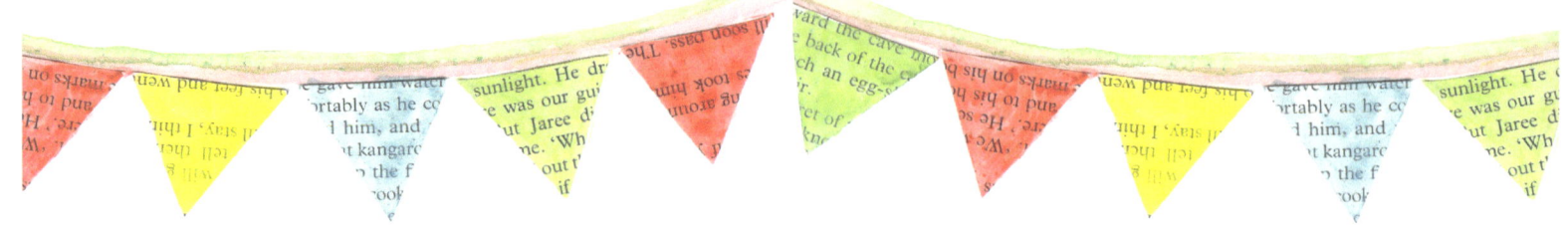

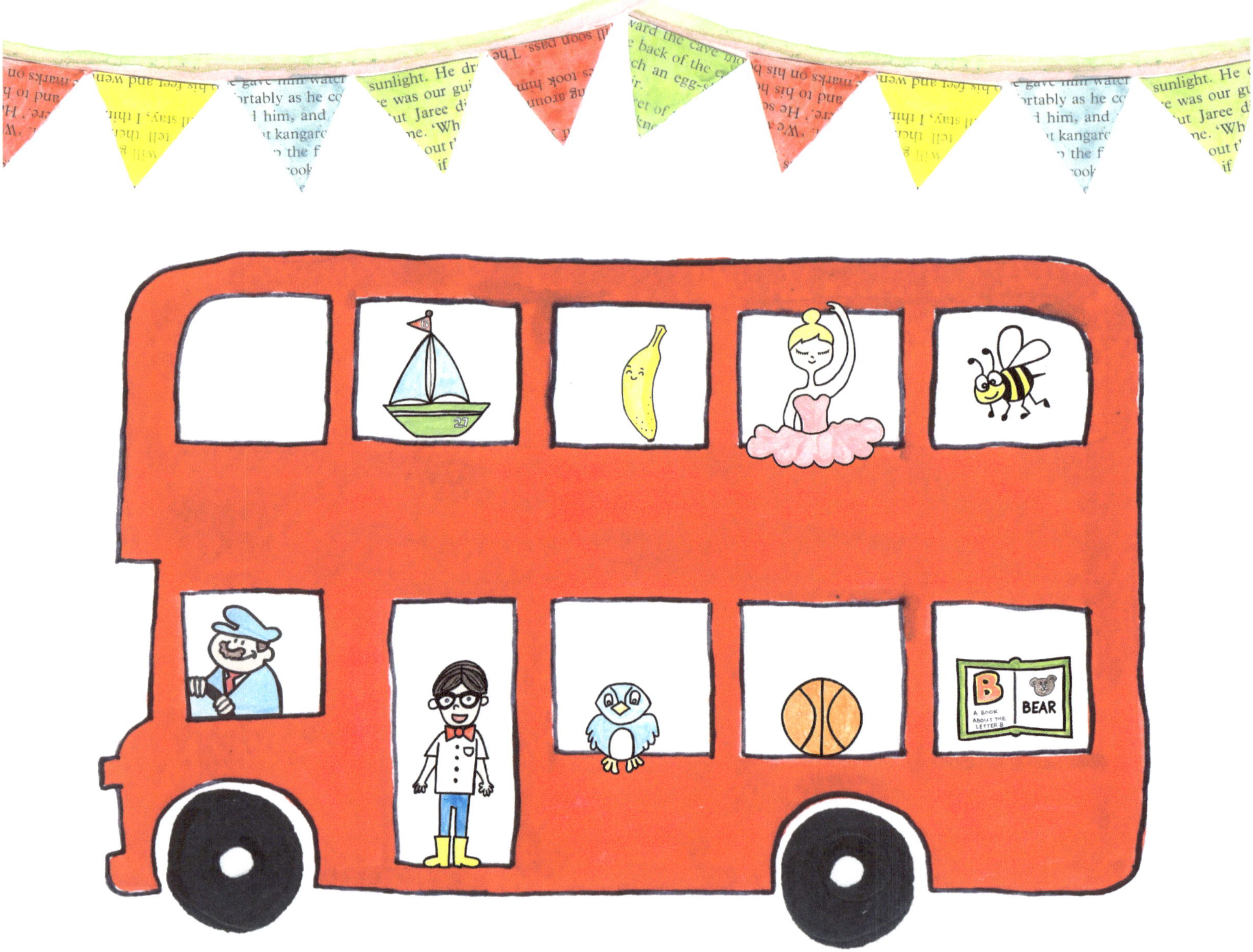

There is a boy, a bird, a ball, a book,
a bee, a ballerina, a banana
and a boat on a bus.

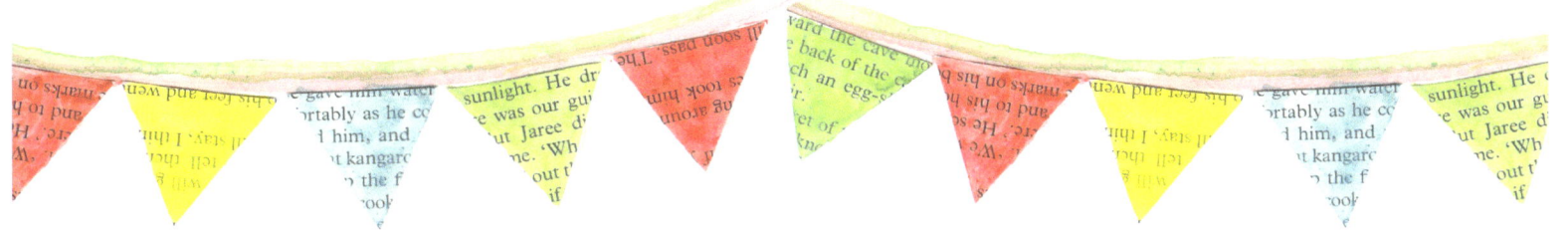

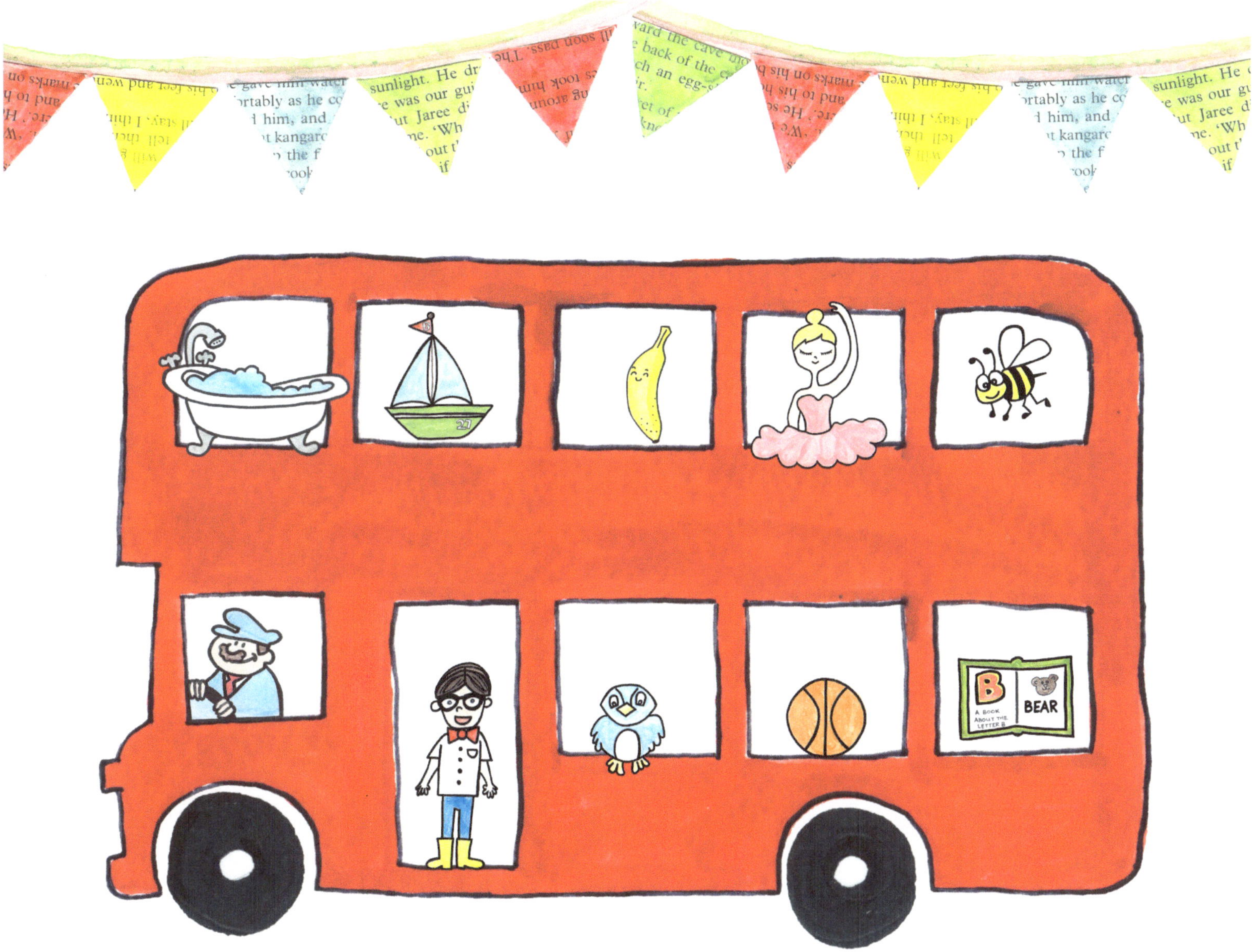

There is a boy, a bird, a ball, a book, a bee, a ballerina, a banana, a boat and a bathtub on a bus.

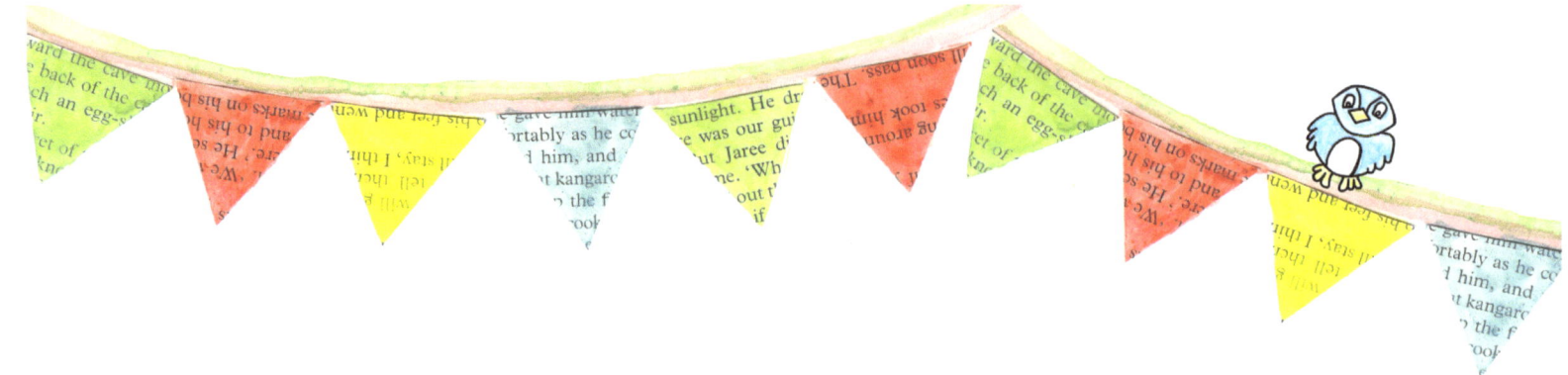

Where are they all going?

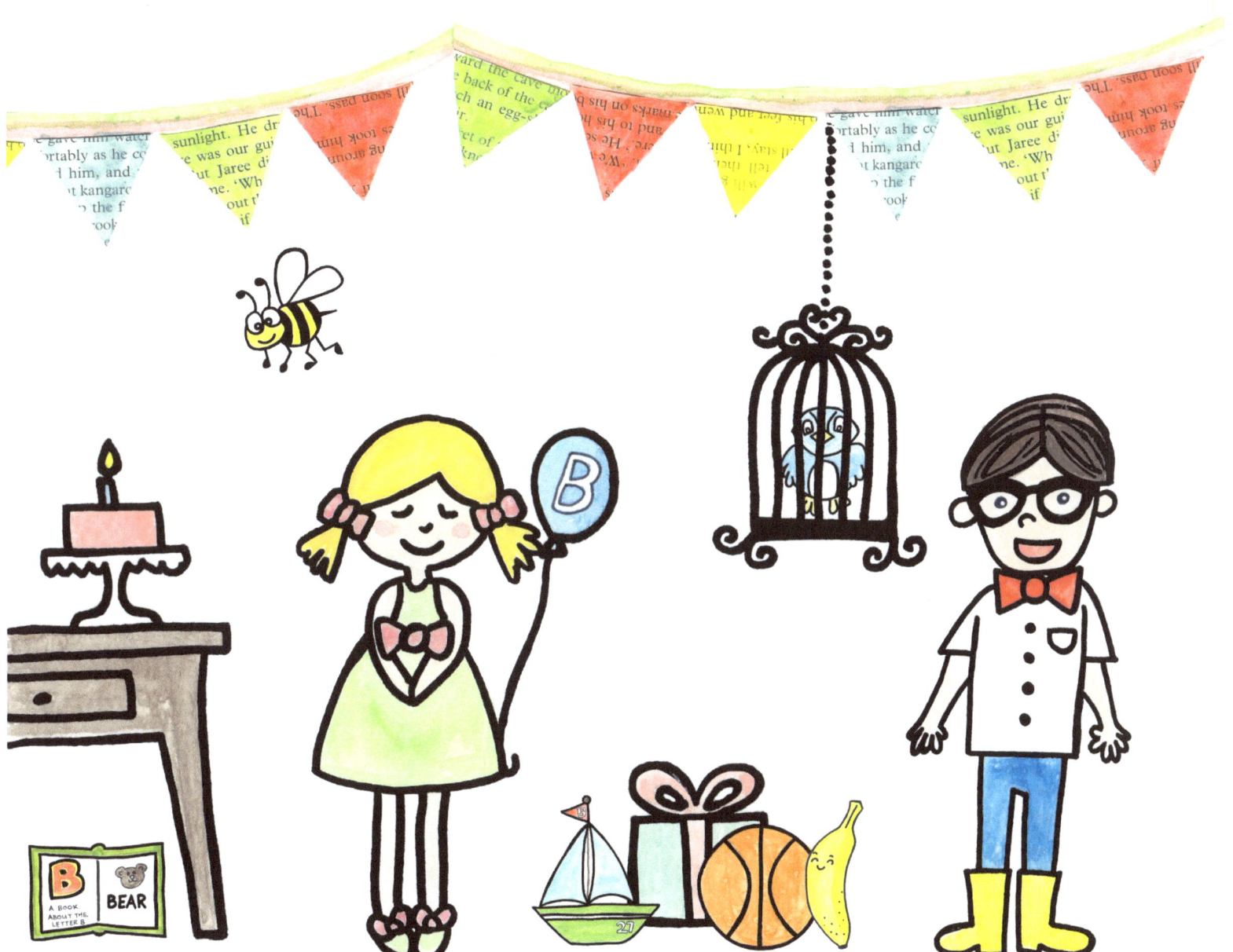

To Beatrice's birthday party!
Can you find all of the things that start with the letter B?

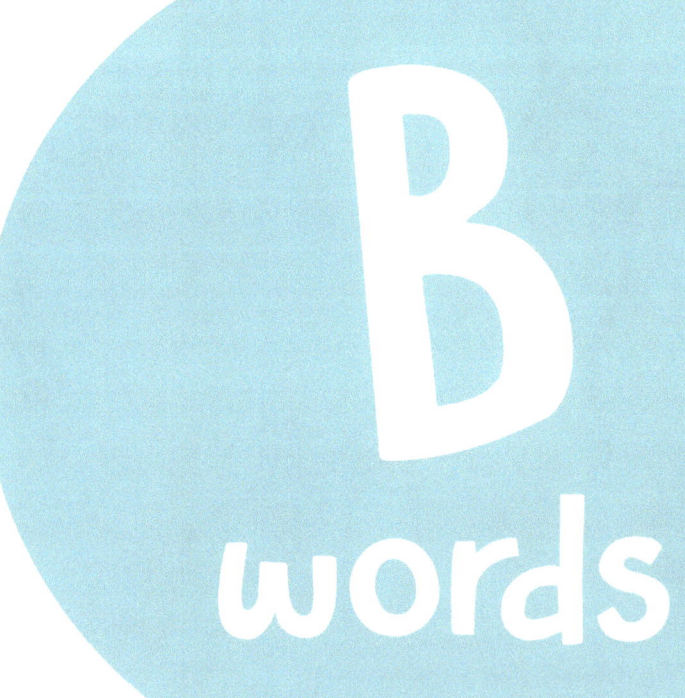

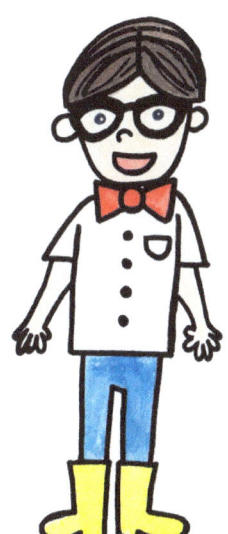

boy

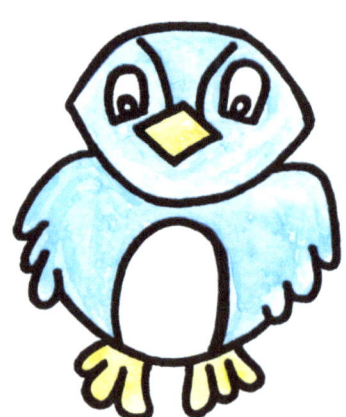

bird

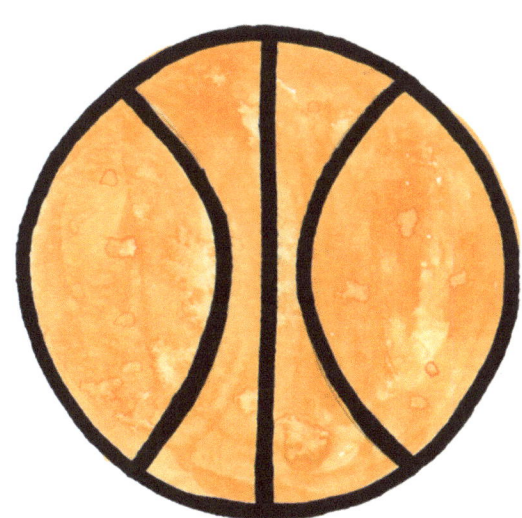

ball

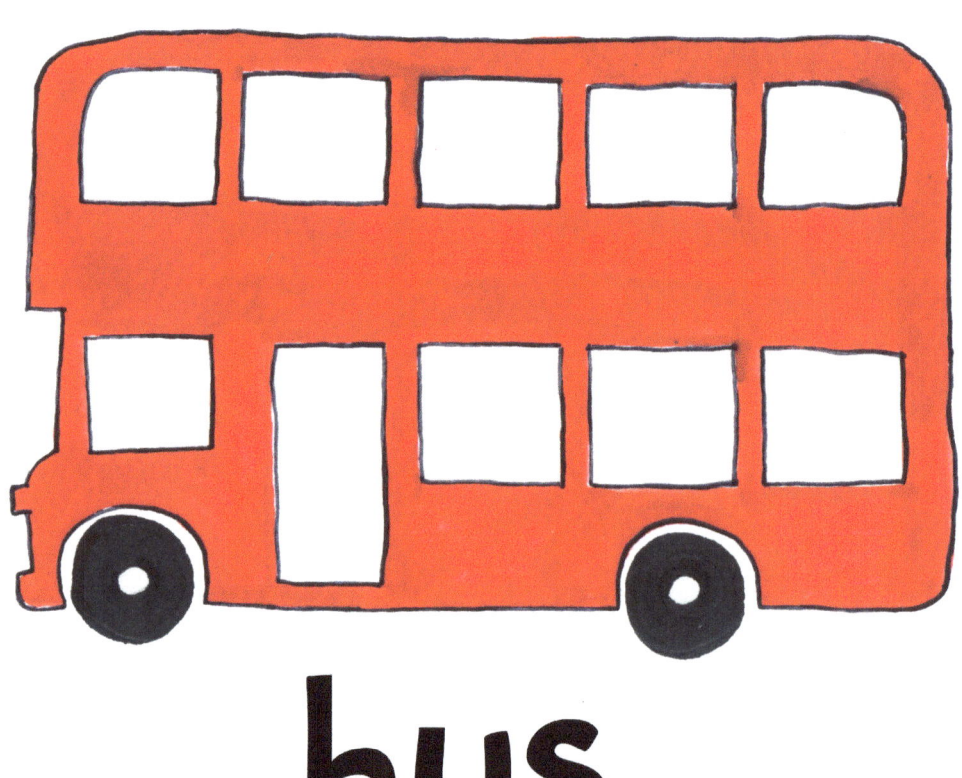

bus

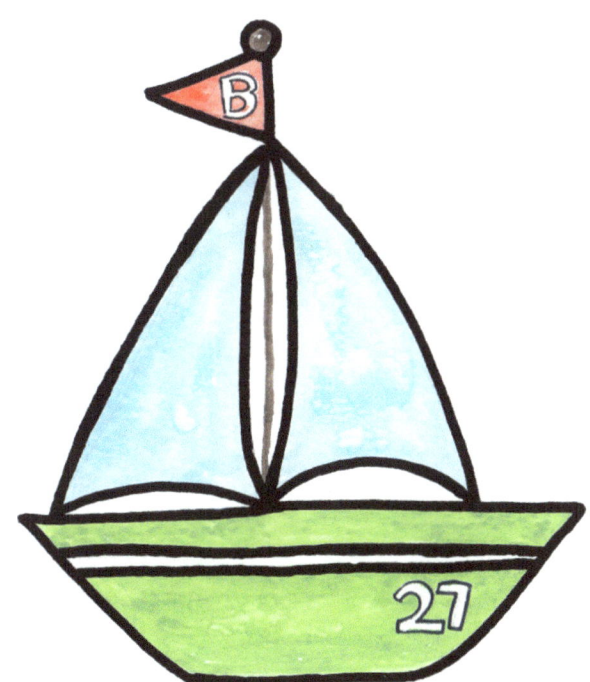

boat

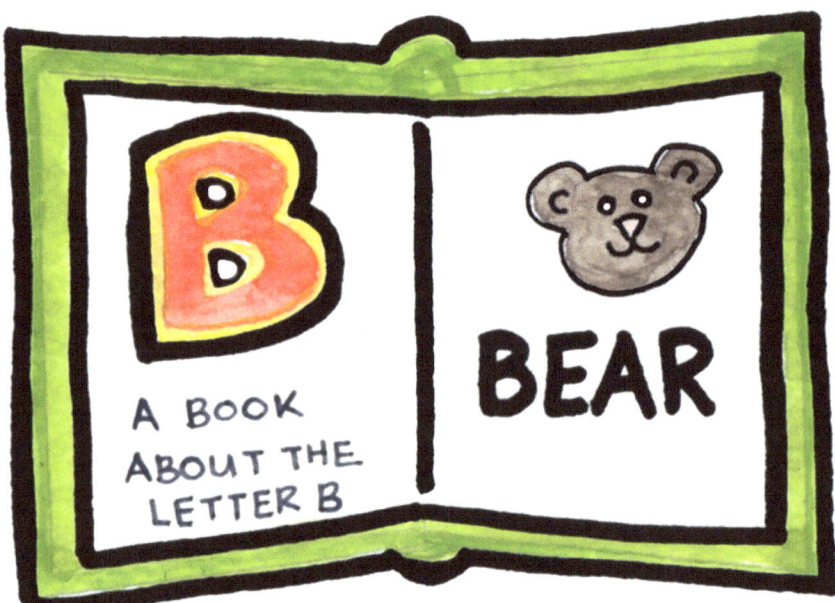

book

bee

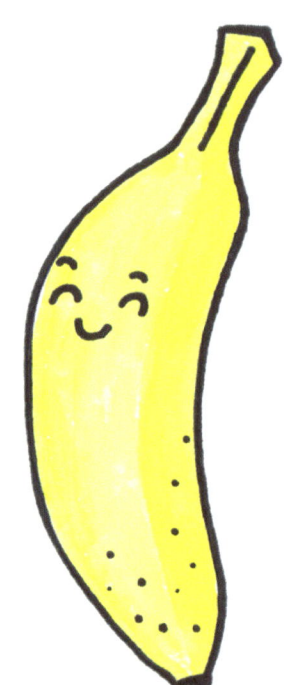

banana

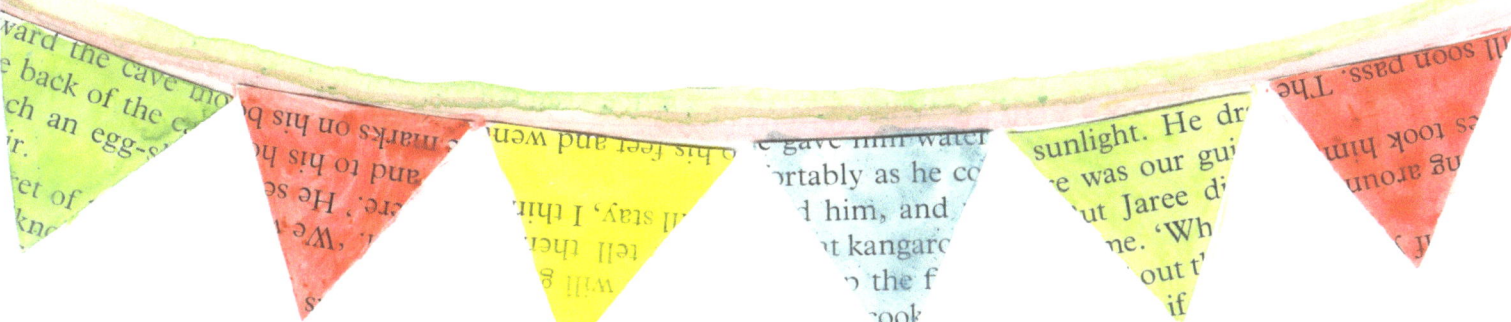
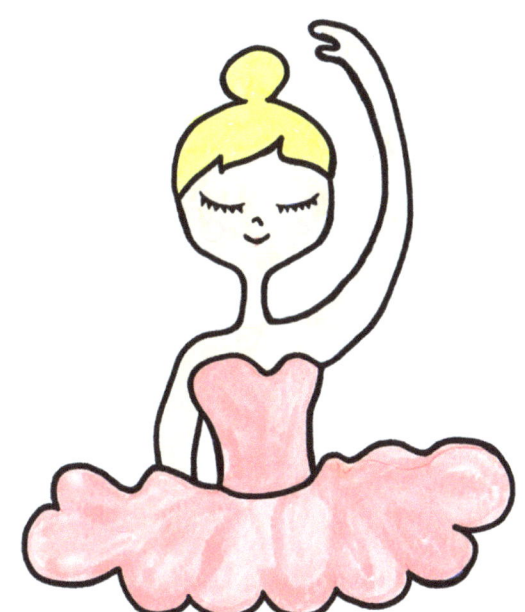

ballerina

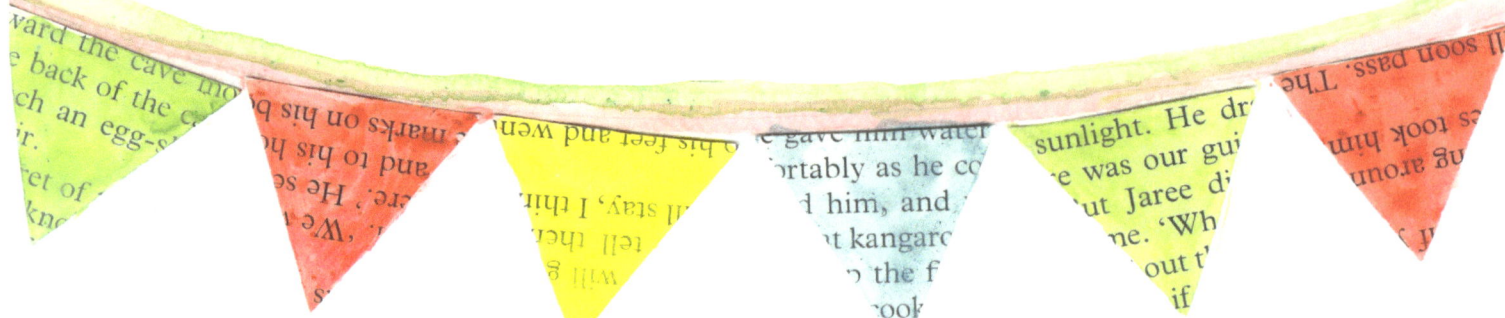
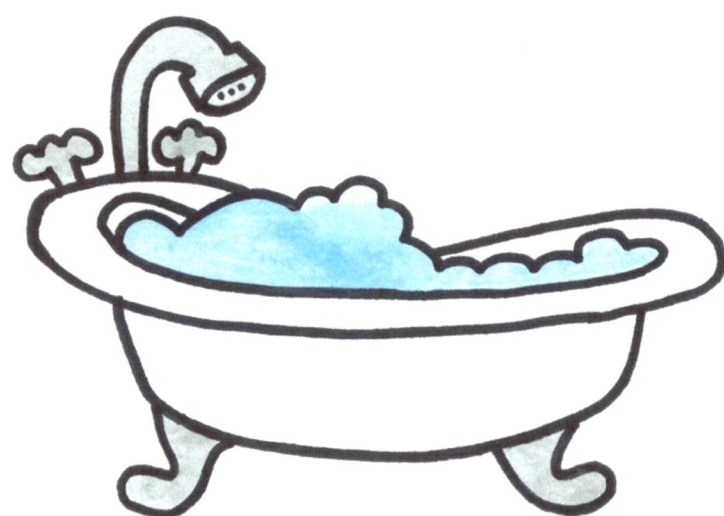

bathtub

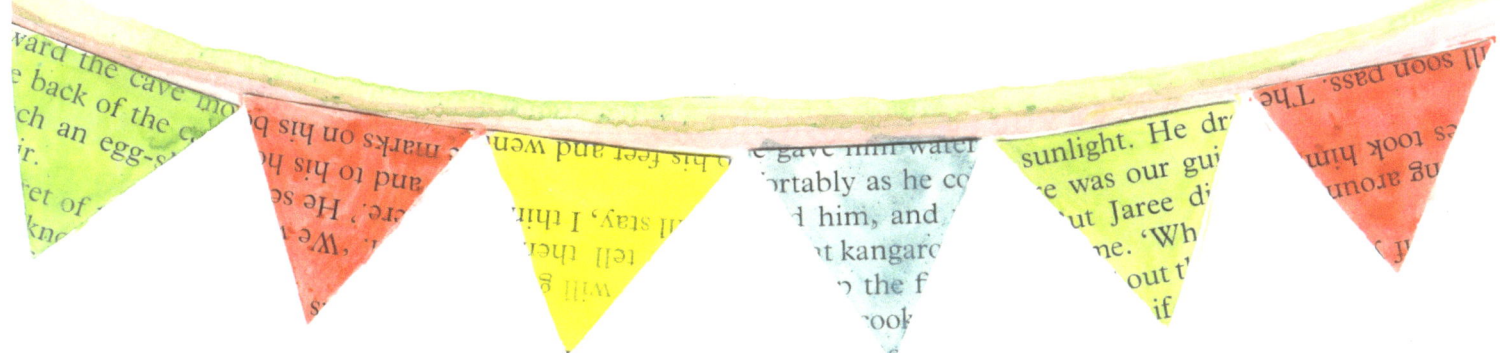
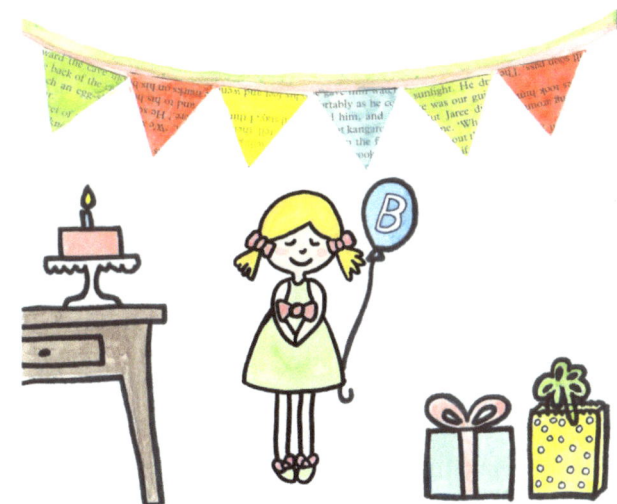

birthday

This book was made using "B Words"!

B is for BLACK marker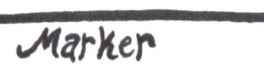

B is for paint BRUSH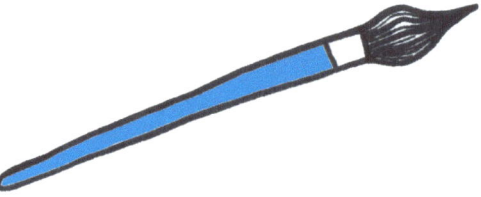

B is for BOOK page

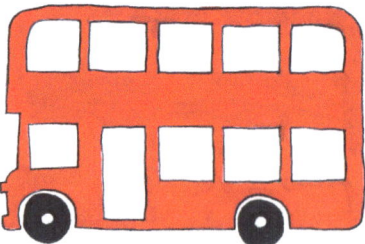

Make your own Boy on a Bus

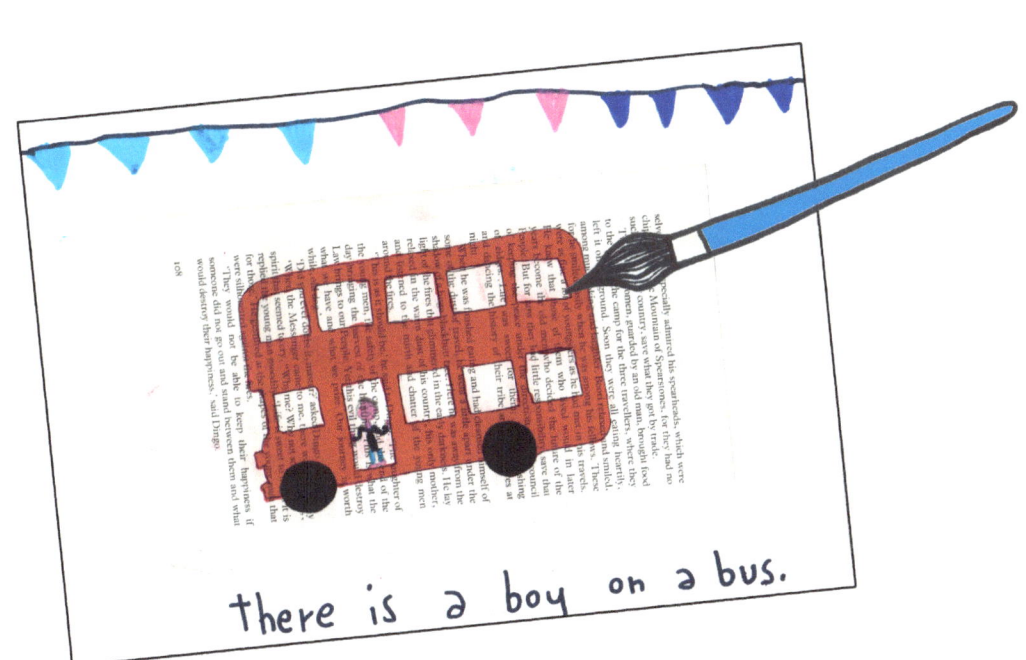

Trace the outline of a bus using a
black marker onto an old book page.
Then fill it in using red paint and a paint brush!

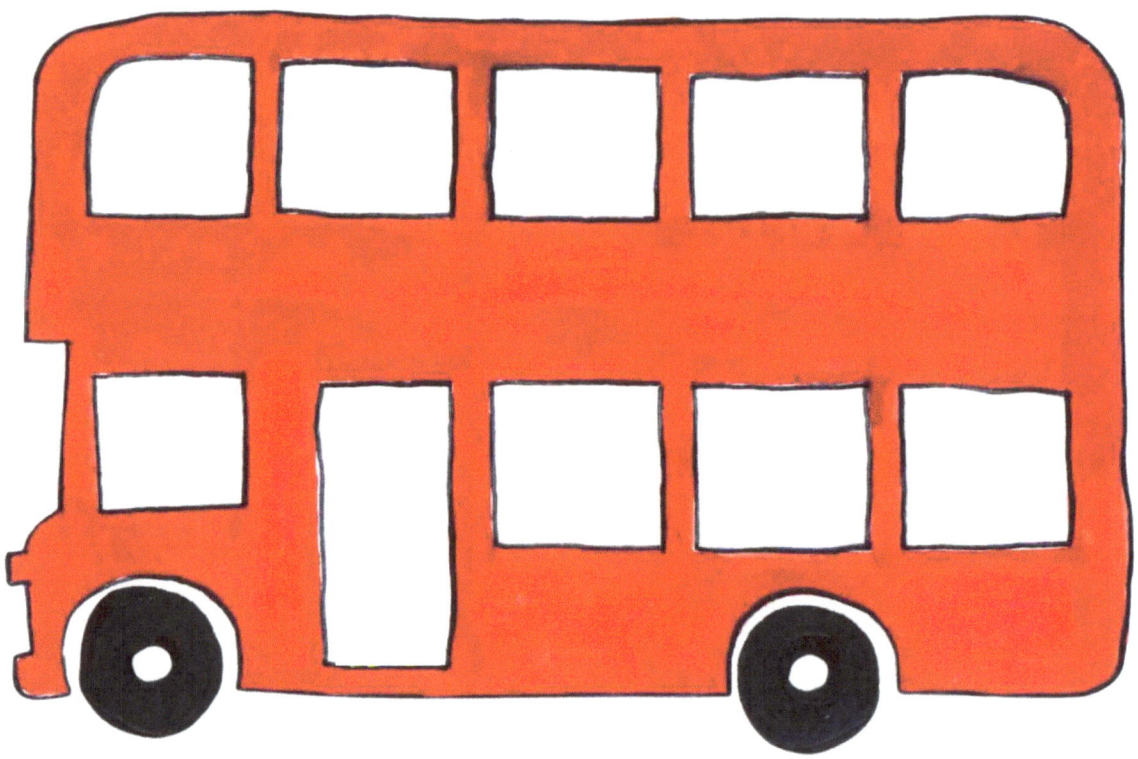

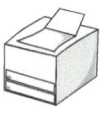 Make a photocopy of this page onto cardstock. Cut out around the outside of the bus and the windows. Then use it as an outline to trace onto a book page.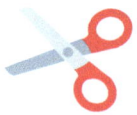

B

This book's
LETTER ACTION

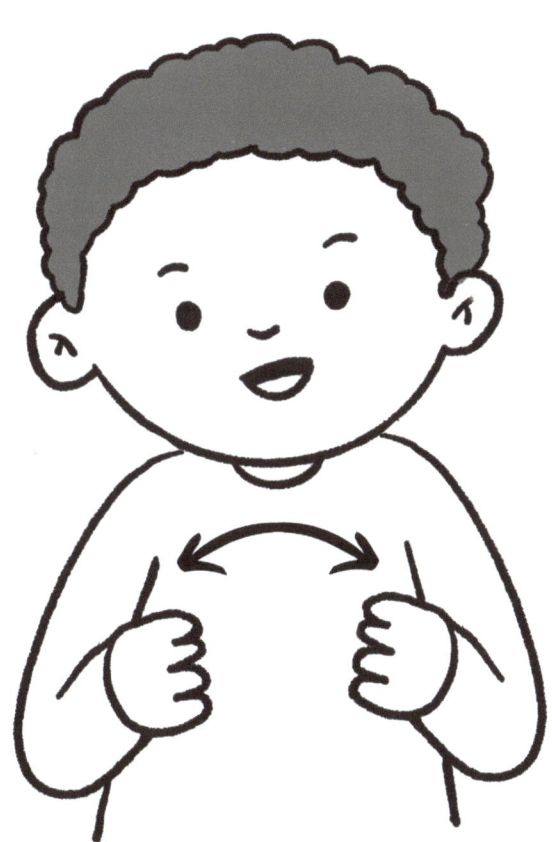

Pretend to drive a bus with both hands on the wheel and say: "b, b, bus"

UDL and H.P. Gentileschi

At H.P. Gentileschi Publishing House, we create all our books and resources using the Universal Design for Learning (UDL) inclusive principle. The goal of UDL is to provide multiple means of teaching methods and materials to remove any barriers to learning and give all children equal opportunities to grow.

For this reason, you will find our books in numerous media forms:
- In print on paperback with easy-to-read fonts and not overly busy illustrations
- Digital eBooks on Amazon Kindle
- Audiobooks linked to each book with QR codes

Our books also come with fun experiential learning activities, such as Letter Actions and craft projects that provide physical movement options that reinforce the book's teaching objectives.

These UDL resources can be helpful for all kids, including English Language Learners and kids with diverse learning and attention abilities. Our book and curriculum characters represent the beautiful diversity that is found in our world, so every child feels included.

AlphaBOX Book Series

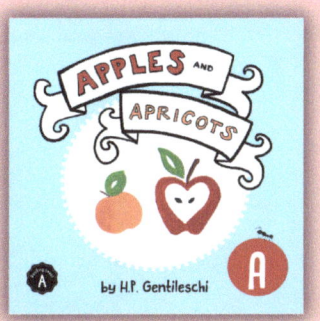
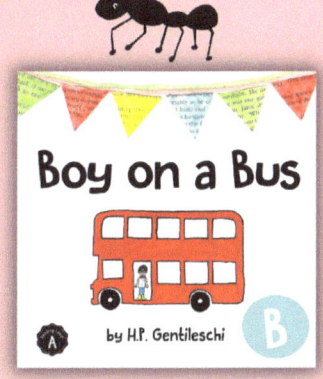
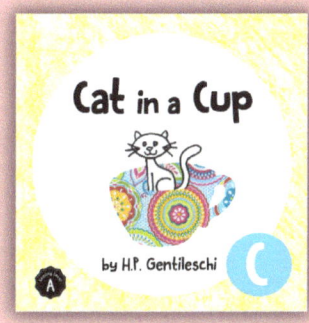
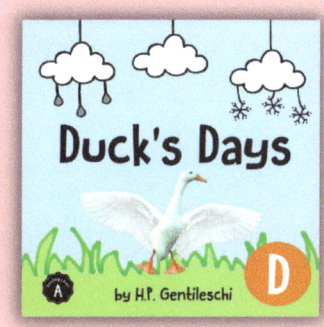
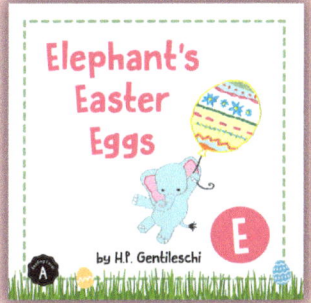
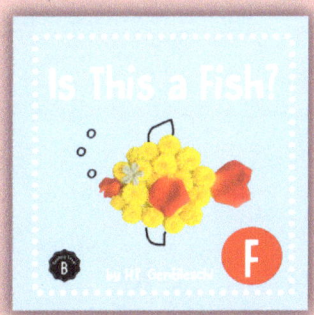
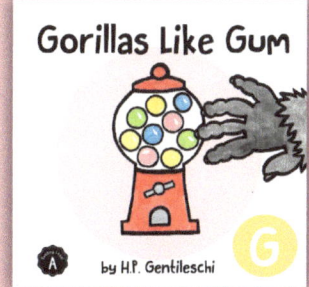
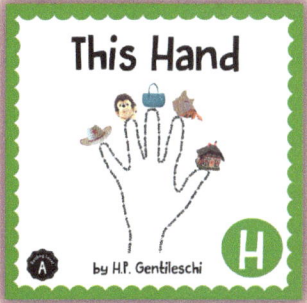
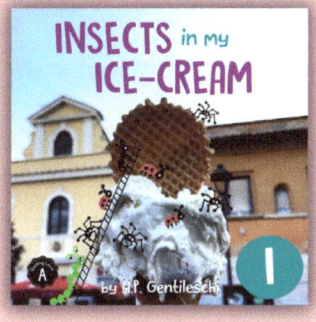
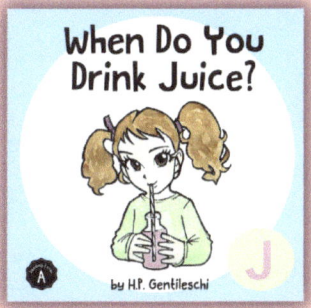
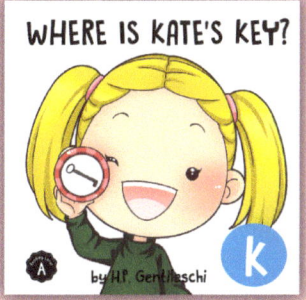
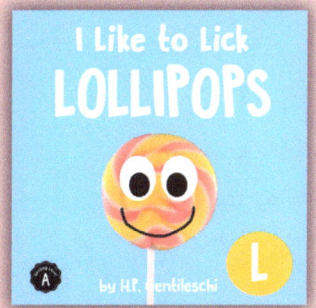

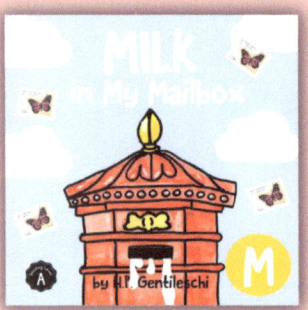
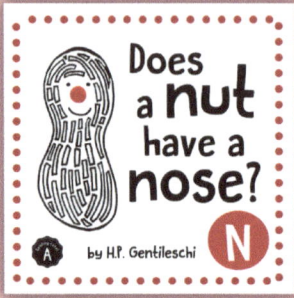
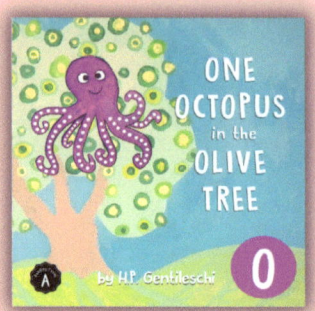
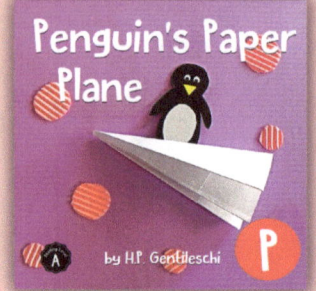
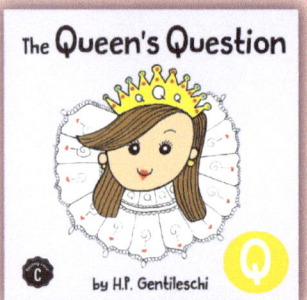
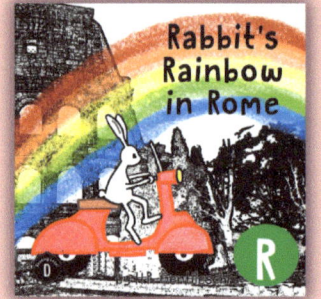
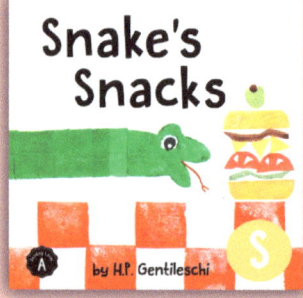
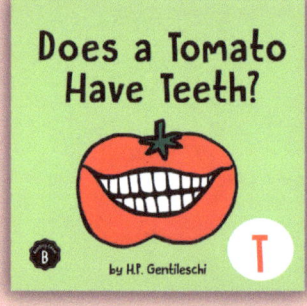
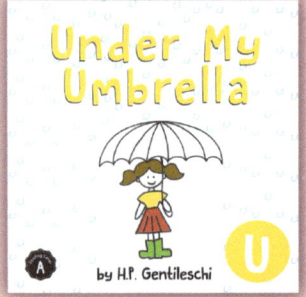
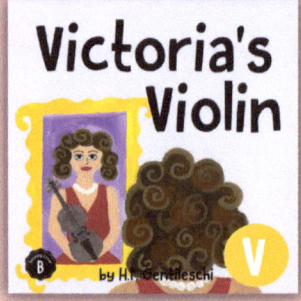
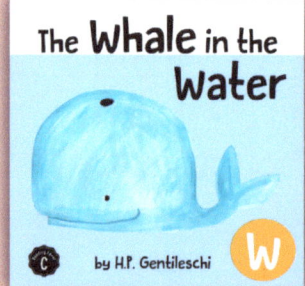
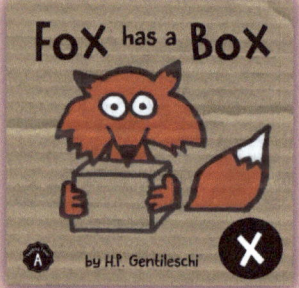
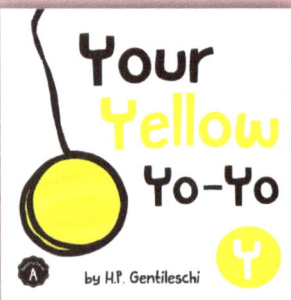
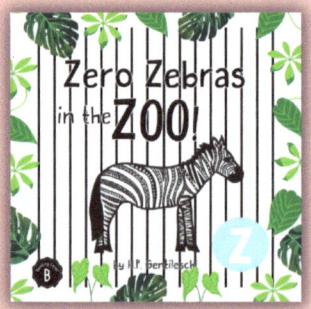
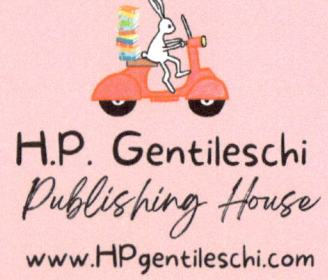

H.P. Gentileschi Publishing House
www.HPgentileschi.com

For all of our Letter Names actions, visit our website!
www.hpgentileschi.com

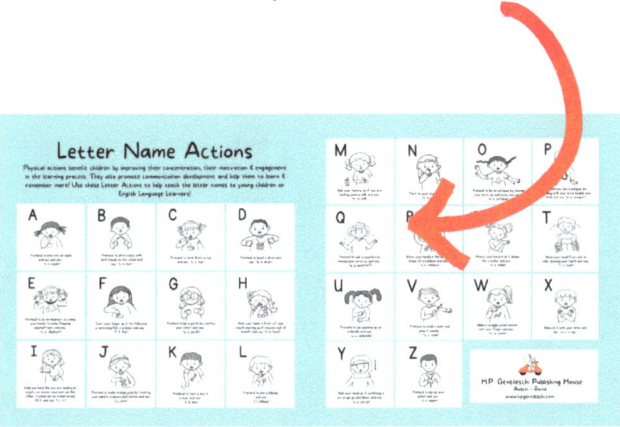

2024 © H.P. Gentileschi Publishing House LLC. All rights reserved. No part of this publication may be reproduced, stored in a retrieval system, or transmitted in any form or by any means, electronic, mechanical, photocopying, recording, or otherwise without the prior permission of the publisher.

The name H.P. Gentileschi and the device are Trade Marks of H.P. Gentileschi Publishing House LLC.

Educators and librarians, for a variety of teaching tools, visit www.hpgentileschi.com

Printed in the U.S.A.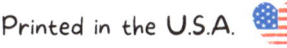

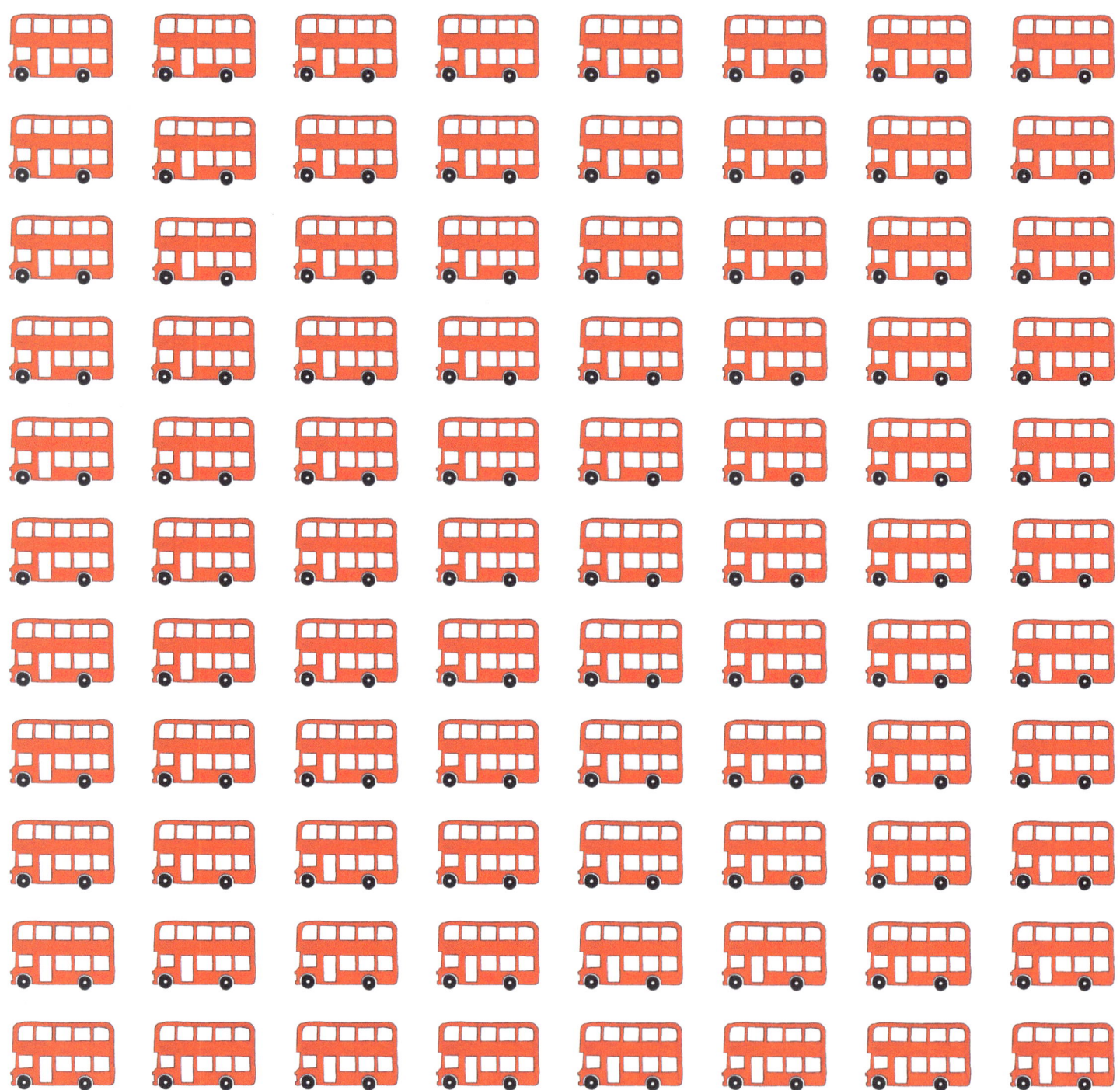

www.ingramcontent.com/pod-product-compliance
Lightning Source LLC
Chambersburg PA
CBHW051840210526
45473CB00005B/1958